OXFORD ENGLISH

QUEST

Y3/P4

PUPIL BOOK 1

KATE RUTTLE

Contents

1 Wildlife Everywhere page 4

2 A History of Ships page 14

3 Egg Buggies and Aunt Maude page 22

Look for these icons so you know what to do.

All the activities are colour coded.
You will all be able to have a go at the **green** activities.

Most of you can do the **orange** activities.

Some of you can do the **red** activities.

Think it!

Just because you are quiet when you think, it doesn't mean you're not working! Think about the question carefully, and be ready to talk about your answer. There's often no right or wrong.

Say it!

For these activities you will need to say your answer, or discuss what you think. Make sure you have thought about what you want to say before you speak. Don't forget to listen too! You will need to work with a friend, or in a small group.

Write it!

For these activities you will need to write things down, so make sure you have a pen or pencil and paper. Before you write, decide whether you need to write in notes, or in your best handwriting.

4 Far, Far Away, Many Years Ago   page 32

5 From the Ends of the Earth   page 42

6 A B-to-T of Body Bits   page 52

Writing mats   page 62

Draw it!

For these activities you will need pencils or pens for drawing. Think about the reason for your drawing before you start. Is it to make something look better, or to make something clearer to someone else?

Enjoy it?

This icon asks you to think whether you have enjoyed what you have read. Think about what you liked – and what you didn't!

Act it!

This icon tells you that you will need to act these activities. You will need to work with a friend, or in a small group.

p.4–19

This icon tells you which pages in the Companion to look at to answer the question.

This icon tells you helpful things.

Enjoy it?

p.4-19 Did you enjoy reading about 'Wildlife Everywhere' in unit 1 of the Companion? Which was your favourite bit? Why?

Sort it!

Wildlife text types

p.4-19 In 'Wildlife Everywhere' in the Companion there are different types of text, to tell you different types of things.

Which text type is each of these?

Choose from:

- narrative (story);
- recount (retelling something that happened to you);
- report (giving information about something);
- instructions (telling you how to do something);
- poetry.

When you have finished, try to jot down notes to explain what helped you to make up your mind each time.

In your book:

If you think that sentence 1 is a report text type, write ...

1 = report
2 =

1. Some common garden birds are disappearing from gardens and parks.

2. Glue all the pieces together, as shown.

3. A Bee!
A Bee!
Is after me!!!

4. "Ghosts, Granpa," Skip shivered.
"I can hear them late at night –"

5. Mum got cross with me for leaving my shoes outside, but I think the fox got into the kitchen and took my shoe out through the cat flap.

Punctuate it!

City wildlife

Lots of birds, insects and animals have moved into towns and cities. Read this paragraph about birds that live in towns and cities. Then copy the paragraph, adding capital letters and full stops to make sentences. (You will need five capital letters and five full stops.)

lots of birds now live in cities in the country birds build nests in tall trees and on cliffs in the city birds also build nests on high buildings cities are often more noisy than the country some city birds have begun to sing louder so they can hear each other over the noise of the traffic

Get it?

Fact finding

Use unit 1 of the Companion to find answers to these questions and write them in sentences.

p.4 Introduction

1. Which creature lives in a colony in a hollow tree?
2. Which creature lives in damp places?
3. What kind of creature is a Brown Hairstreak?
4. Which creature eats sugary things?
5. What do snails eat?
6. Which are the least common creatures in the chart?

Expand it!

p.4 Write eight proper sentences to give some of the information in the chart on page 4 of the Companion.

p.12–17 Foxes, bats and birds

1. What do you think is the main reason why foxes are moving away from the countryside?
2. Why do urban foxes live for a shorter time than foxes in the countryside?
3. Why should you make a bat box?
4. Which is the smallest bat in Britain?
5. Which do you think is the main reason why bird numbers are going down? Try to explain why.
6. What food can you put out for birds?

Feeding garden birds

In *Disappearing garden birds* on pages 16 and 17 of the Companion, you read about how the numbers of garden birds are falling. One way to help garden birds to live is to put food out for them.

The table shows what kind of food to give to different types of birds.

Type of bird	Kind of food	Where to feed
Greenfinches and tits	Nuts	Metal hanging nut feeders (plastic mesh feeders can trap birds' feet)
	Coconut shell filled with fat	Hanging
	Balls of fat mixed with seeds and fruit	Hanging (beware of squirrels stealing it!)
Thrushes and dunnocks	Bread, seed	Scatter on the ground (beware of cats and rats!)
Perching birds, e.g. blackbirds, finches, buntings and sparrows	Seeds, fat, fruit	Bird table

The first question could be:

① What do thrushes and dunnocks eat?

Here are some answers to questions you could ask about the information in the table. You need to write the questions! (Don't forget to use a question mark.)

1 They eat bread and seed.

2 They eat on bird tables.

3 Thrushes and dunnocks eat here.

4 Squirrels might steal the food.

5 Greenfinches eat them.

6 Plastic feeders can trap birds' feet.

Get it?

p.18–19 Look at the poems on pages 18 and 19 of the Companion. Find answers to these questions and write them in sentences.

Poems

1. Who lives by the curb stone?
2. What has the spider got coiled up inside her?
3. Why did the poet let the butterfly go?
4. How did Spike Milligan feel about the bee?
5. Write five sets of rhyming words from different poems.
6. Which creatures did the poets admire?

Fox action

Get into groups of five.

p.9–10 Reread the passage in the story *Live and Let Live* on pages 9 and 10 of the Companion, where Skip and Grandpa first notice the fox near to Poppy (beginning, 'Skip could see what Granpa meant).

Each person in the group needs to take a role: Director; Skip; Granpa; Poppy; Fox.

Director, watch while the others mime the action until the moment when Skip sees the fox, then call "Freeze frame!" Immediately, everyone must freeze, thinking about:

⊙ the expression on their face;
⊙ what they were in the middle of doing – their body will have to show this.

Director, look at the scene for a moment, then choose one of the characters to take over from. Your face and body have to fit into the 'freeze frame' moment.

The new Director calls "Action" and the characters mime the action again.

The new Director then calls "Freeze frame!" and immediately, everyone must freeze.

New Director, you look at the scene, then take over from a different character.

Carry on like this until everyone has had a turn at being the Director and being a character.

Then discuss:

⊙ how you knew how each of the characters was feeling;
⊙ how you decided which expression to wear;
⊙ whether you felt that everyone else had a good body posture. What could have been improved?

Live and Let Live

p.5–11 You've read the story *Live and Let Live* in unit 1 of the Companion. What did you think about it?

Story summary

Talk to your group about the story. Think about:

⊙ *the plot* – did you enjoy it? Use words from the story as part of your answer.
⊙ *the characters* – did you believe in them? Use words from the story as part of your answer.
⊙ *the setting* – was it well described? Use words from the story as part of your answer.
⊙ *the dialogue* – did you like reading a story with so much dialogue? Use words from the story as part of your answer.

Prepare to talk to the rest of the class about the story. Plan what you're going to say.

Write it!

Fox playscript

Choose a short extract from the story
Live and Let Live in unit 1 of the
Companion and rewrite it as a playscript.
Use words from the story.

You might want to begin
like this:

On the way home from
school
Skip (softly): Granpa ...

Remember that in a playscript:

- you don't use speech marks. Write the
  name of the character and the words
  they say;
- you can tell the actors how to say a line
  by putting an adverb in brackets;
- you need to begin by telling your actors
  where the action is taking place.

Describe it!

Story settings

Look at these pictures of possible story settings. Choose the one you think could be the setting for the most interesting story and write a paragraph describing it.

The Poor Snail

p.18 Read the poem *The Poor Snail* on page 18 of the Companion. Draw a picture to match the poem.

Think about these questions:

How much like a real snail should your picture be? Is this meant to be a real snail or a 'story' snail? How do you know? How much detail do you need to add so that people know that you are drawing this snail, not a different snail in a different poem?

Say it

Learn it!

Wildlife poem

p.18–19 Choose one of the poems on pages 18 and 19 of the Companion or the poem *Wasps*, on the opposite page. Say it over and over to yourself until you remember the whole poem. Prepare to perform it to the class. Think about how you can use expression to make the poem more interesting for your audience.

Wasps

Wasps like
coffee.

Syrup.

Tea.

Coca-cola.

Butter.

Me.

Dorothy Aldis

Verb hunt

There is at least one verb in every sentence.

Find the verb in each of these sentences and write it down.

In your book, write:

① = lives

② =

1. An ant lives in a big group.
2. Badgers live in setts.
3. Bats roost in trees.
4. Bee-keepers keep honey bees.
5. Foxes eat food from dustbins.
6. Squirrels climb trees.
7. Wasps sting people!
8. I don't like spiders.
9. Butterflies are adult caterpillars.
10. Snails have hard shells.

Debate it!

Choose one of these opinions to debate. Decide whether you agree or disagree – remember, you will have to explain why you think what you think.

We should chase foxes away from our houses and gardens. They make too much noise and mess and they might attack children.

I don't like having bats in my attic because they destroy my roof.

I won't tell anyone that they are there. I'll just frighten them away.

There are fewer garden birds than there were because squirrels eat their eggs. I know this because I saw a squirrel eating a bird's eggs.

Shorten it!

p.13 Read the diary extract on page 13 of the Companion. Think about the main idea. Retell the story in two sentences.

A History of Ships

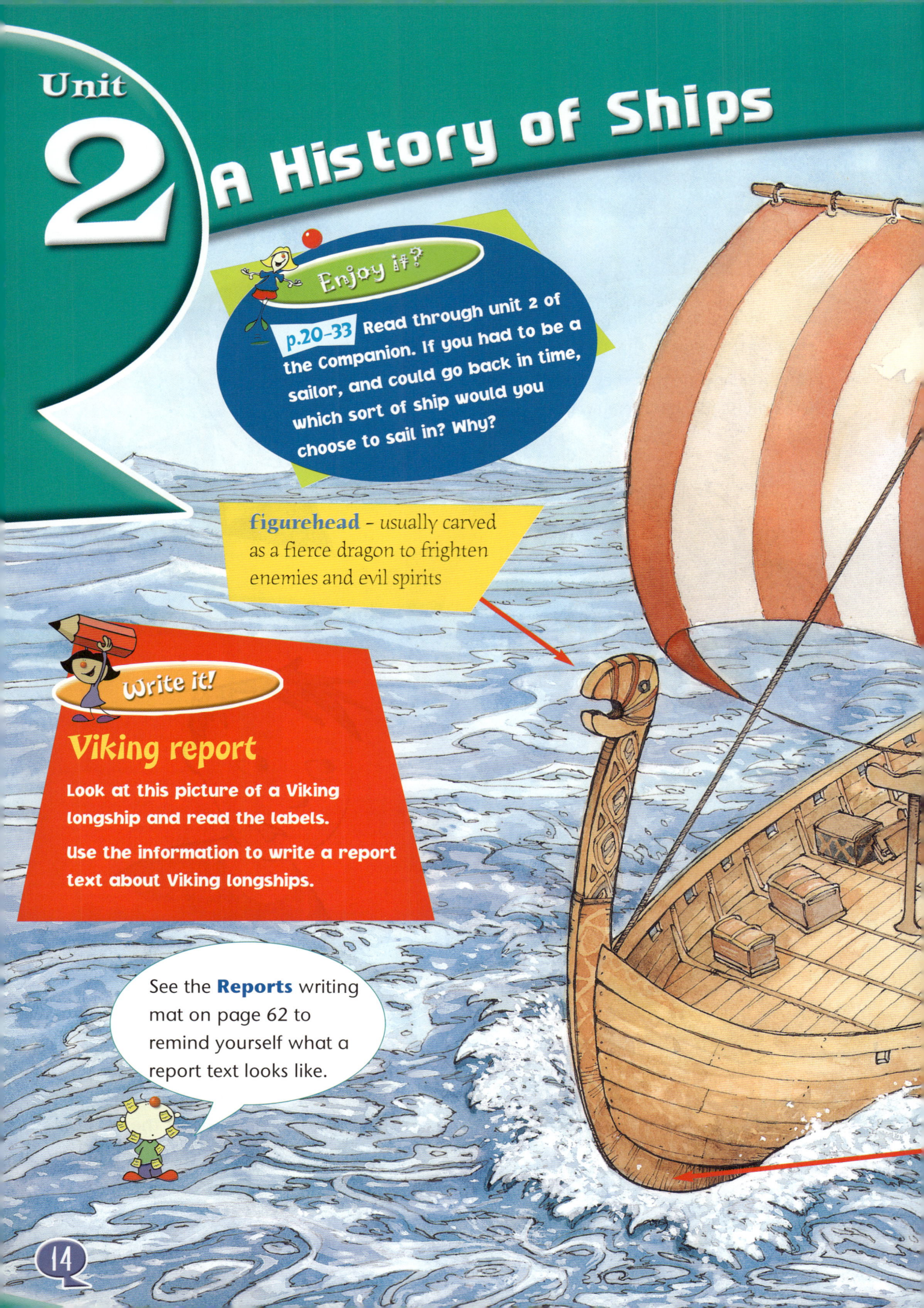

Enjoy it?

p.20-33 Read through unit 2 of the Companion. If you had to be a sailor, and could go back in time, which sort of ship would you choose to sail in? Why?

figurehead – usually carved as a fierce dragon to frighten enemies and evil spirits

Write it!

Viking report

Look at this picture of a Viking longship and read the labels.

Use the information to write a report text about Viking longships.

See the **Reports** writing mat on page 62 to remind yourself what a report text looks like.

tall pine **mast**

sail – large, square, often coloured

side rudder (styri) – oak paddle for steering

water barrel – storage of drinking water

oar storage – for when sail is used

seaman's chest – sailor's belongings and rowing seat

oar ports – allow oars to be used to row ship when no wind

keel –
- made of oak
- very shallow to allow travel up rivers
- light to allow for transport over land

Sort it!

Viking text type match

Match the texts 1–4 below to the text types.
Write another sentence to continue each text.

In your book, write:
1 =
2 =

A instruction text

B recount

C fiction

D report

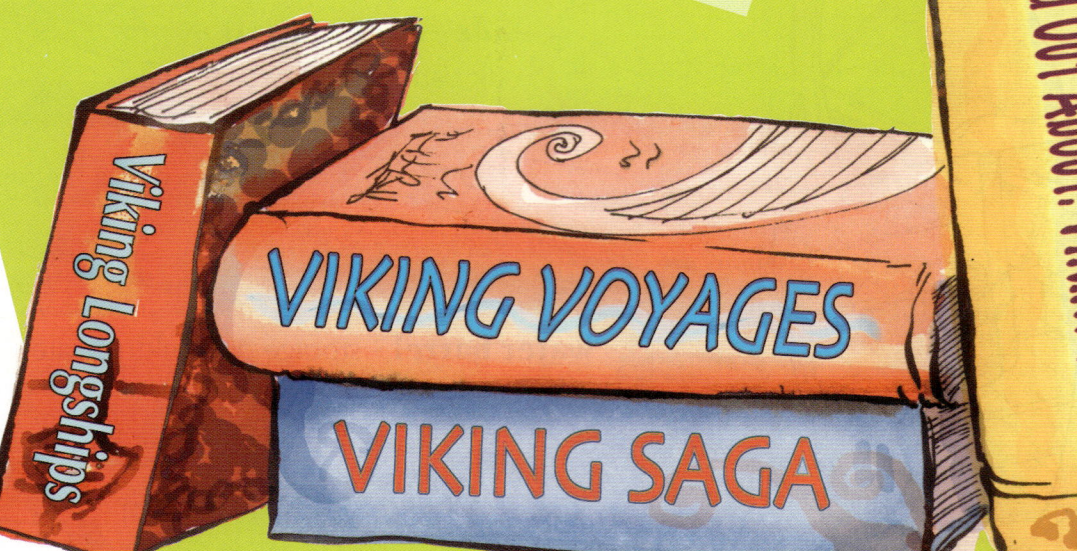

1 Longships were the Viking warships. They were light, but strong, and could carry up to 32 Viking pirates.

2 One day, a poor old bondi (freedman) was waiting a long time for his mate while all the other boats rowed out as each was ready. Then, …

3 I travelled from Hedeby to Truso in seven days, sailing both day and night. Wendland was on my starboard, and on the port side were other lands belonging to Denmark.

4 Compare a modern warship with a Viking longship.

Find out about where Vikings got the wood to build their boats.

Viking facts

Rewrite this passage, adding punctuation.
(You will need three capital letters, four full stops and two commas.)

Viking ships ruled the seas for more than 300 years they were faster and more seaworthy than any other ships that existed at the time the most famous Viking ship was the longship which was light strong and ideal for surprise raids the Viking shipbuilders used only very simple tools and had no plans to help them relying entirely on their hands and eyes

Think it

Think it!

Party on the Golden Hinde

p.24 Read about Molly's night on the *Golden Hinde* on page 24 of the Companion. Would you have liked to be at the party?

In your group, decide what you think would have been the best bit about the party, and which would have been the worst.

Find it!

Fact finding: the *Mary Rose*

p.25–27 **Find out about the *Mary Rose* using pages 25–27 of the Companion. Write the answers in your book.**

1 When was the *Mary Rose* built?

2 Which king was reigning when it was built?

3 What was the main change in the design of the *Mary Rose*?

4 Name three features of the *Mary Rose*.

5 Find two materials which were used in the building of the ship. What was each one used for?

6 When was the *Mary Rose* sunk?

7 Who was the enemy in the war in which the *Mary Rose* was sunk?

8 Where was she sunk?

9 Why do you think the *Mary Rose* sank?

10 How many people were rescued when she sank?

Compare it!

Ship design

p.25–27 **Copy and fill in the table to show good and bad things about Tudor ship design. Use information from pages 25–27 of the Companion.**

Design	Good or bad? Why?
Ships relied on wind power and had square sails.	
Guns on top decks at the front and back of the ship.	
Carvel-made hulls	
Guns closer to the waterline	

Change it!

Tudor tenses

p.25-27 **In your book, write:**

	Present tense	Past tense
①	help	helped

You can find passages about the *Mary Rose* with the past or the present tense of all these verbs on pages 25–27 of the Companion.

Present tense	Past tense	Present tense	Past tense
want	1	lead	11
lift	2	12	fought
3	attacked	13	meant
4	saved	have	14
is	5	15	overcrowded
6	sank	win	16
want	7	order	17
8	came	18	relied
give	9	19	built
10	were	20	tried

Act it!

Sinking sailors

p.26-27 **Imagine you are sailors on the *Mary Rose* when she starts to sink. Before you act it, discuss:**

- How would you feel? Would you be scared? Worried? Calm, because you didn't think the ship would sink?
- How would the ship move under your feet? Practise moving in that way.
- What would you say? And in what kind of voice? Would you ask an officer for orders? Talk to your ship mates? Ignore everyone and concentrate on saving yourself? Would you shout? Scream? Whisper?

Mime it!

Mary Lacy

p.28–31 In your group, read the story of Mary Lacy in unit 2 of the Companion. Choose one or two of the episodes to mime. Can the others guess which episode you chose?

You could act:

- Mary falling into the ship's hold, banging her head and having it stitched;
- Mary falling into the sea while trying to get onto the *Royal William*;
- Mary hobbling around on her spiked crutches;
- or any other episode.

Say it

Biography v recount

Are biographies like recount texts? Features of a recount text are:

Purpose: — to retell events

Organisation or structure:
— opening which sets the scene
— events listed in the order they happened
— closing statement, which tells you how the event ended

Language:
— written in the first person (*I*)
— written in the past tense (*I went*)
— connectives that signal time passing (e.g. *later, then, seven years passed*)
— written about one person, or a group of people

Discuss how biographies and recounts are the same and different.

The good ship Sandwich

p.29-30 In the Companion, read the description of the *Sandwich*, the ship that Mary Lacy first worked on. What do you think it was like in the sick bay? Or where Mary slept? Or on deck of the ship? Draw what you think it was like.

Ship changes over time

Think of as many reasons as you can for boats and ships to change over time.

Think about:

- the materials they are made from;
- the tools people had;
- who built the boats;
- where the boats were to be sailed – in open sea, along coasts, up rivers;
- what the boats were used for.

Now discuss what you think in a small group.

Compare it!

p.20-33 Choose two of these ships. Sketch and label them, then try to list five things that are the same and five that are different. Which list is easier?

Unit 3

Egg Buggies and Aunt Maude

Enjoy it?

p.34–42 Read about egg buggies in 'Egg Buggies and Aunt Maude' in the Companion. Which egg buggy would you like to make? Can you think of any other sorts of egg buggies?

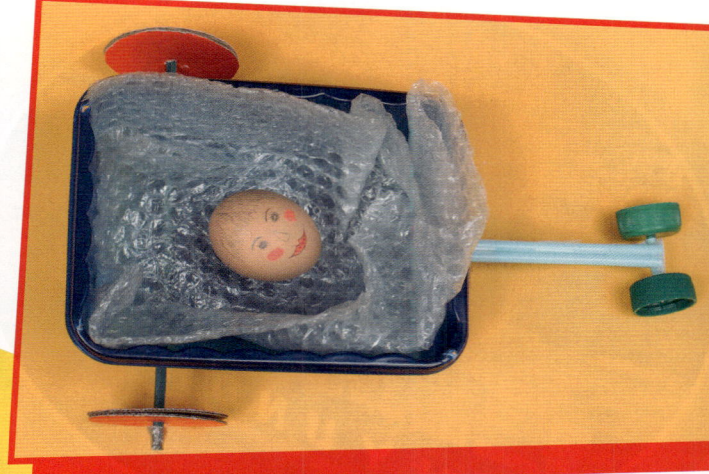

Say it!

Say it

Give me five

In your group, discuss these questions and write the lists:

1 Can you describe an egg? List the five most important adjectives.

2 How would a buggy for carrying eggs be different from one for carrying ping-pong balls or small, round stones? List the five most important ways.

3 What are the main things you need to be careful of when moving eggs around? Why? List the five most important things.

4 Why would anyone want to build a buggy for carrying an egg? List five reasons.

Prepare to tell the rest of the class about your findings.

Instructions, instructions, instructions …

Bits of different instruction texts have been rescued after a fire.

Can you work out what they were written for?

> in the playground.
> ☺ If you are lonely, sit on the friendship bench and someone will come and play with you.
> ☺ Share the toys with the other children.

- The first person who throws a 6 should start.
- Throw the dice.
- Move your counter that number of squares. If you land on a snake, you must go to

10.00 – 10.15	Assembly
10.15 – 10.30	Playtime
10.30 – 11.30	Maths
11.30 – 12.00	Music
12.00 – 1.00	Lunch

1 First, break the eggs into the bowl and whisk them.
2 Then, add the sugar and the butter.
3 Mix all the ingredients together until the mixture looks creamy.
4 Sift the flour. Slowly mix the flour in with the egg, sugar and butter.

SATURDAY 9th APRIL
School Hall
1–3p.m.
Bring and buy
Raffle
Home-made cakes

How would you know that these were all instruction texts? Write down the clues you used.

All mixed up

These are the instructions for making a paper spring.

Rewrite them in the right order, then make the paper spring.

In your book, write:

Instructions for making a paper spring

①

②

etc.

Finally, untape the strips from the table.

You will need: 2 strips of different coloured paper. Each strip should be 30 cm long and 1cm wide. Sticky tape.

Then, fold strip 1 over strip 2 and press down. Next, fold strip 2 over strip 1.

You have made a paper spring.

First, tape one end of strip 1 to the table. Then tape the end of strip 2 so that it is at right angles to strip 1.

Keep going until you have used all of both strips.

strip 1

strip 2

Check your understanding

Reread pages 34–40 of the Companion, then write the answers to these questions in your book. Try to write in sentences.

p.34–37 Spring buggy – finding information

1 What is the aim of the Egg Buggy Distance Challenge?

2 What makes the egg's ride gentler?

3 What do you have to do first?

4 What do you call the stick that joins the wheels together?

5 How do you keep the straws on the bottom of the carton?

6 What are the corks used for?

7 How do you make holes around the edge of the cup from the egg box?

8 What do you put in the holes in the cup?

9 What is the last thing you have to do?

p.38–40 Bubble buggy – thinking about the information

1 Do you need thin or thick cardboard to make a bubble buggy? Why?

2 Does your pencil need to be sharp or blunt? Why?

3 Why does the plant cane need to stick out of the sides of the carton?

4 Should you tape the wheels to the cane or leave them to turn freely? Why?

5 Does your cocktail stick match have to be as long as the cane? Why?

6 Why do you think this is called a bubble buggy?

What's it like?

Look at these lists of some of the things you need to make the buggies.

Make a list of all the adjectives you do not need in a list of 'Things you will need' in an instruction text.

Spring buggy	Bubble buggy
a see-through plastic carton	a blue plastic carton
a white cardboard egg box	a green indoor plant cane
4 metal springs	1 used match
2 pretty straws	3 hollow yellow straws
2 brown corks	brown cardboard
sticky tape	see-through sticky tape

Think about these questions:

Why are some of the adjectives useful and some not useful? What kinds of adjectives are not very useful in instructions?

Make a chart

Read this description of how far four egg buggies travelled.

How would you show this information in a chart or a table? Make a chart in your book.

Jed made a spring buggy. He made his buggy very carefully and the wheels went round easily. His buggy went 130 cm on the floor. Kat's bubble buggy went 150 cm. She thought that it could have gone further, but one of her wheels fell off. Samir also made a bubble buggy, but he hurried too much and his front wheels didn't turn round very well. His buggy only went 30 cm along the floor. Anya and Jess's spring buggy went 120 cm. The wheels were not very even so the buggy didn't go in a straight line.

What if ...?

Which buggy do you think will go further – the spring buggy or the bubble buggy? Why?

Can you think of ways of changing the designs to make the buggies go even further? What do you think would happen if ...

- ⊙ you put different-sized wheels on the buggy?
- ⊙ you put more weight in the buggy?
- ⊙ you used a bigger or smaller carton?
- ⊙ you used a steeper ramp?

Talk about your reasons.

Look at these vehicles. Can you find the springs in each one? Think about these questions:

- ⊙ Why are there springs on these vehicles? What do they do?
- ⊙ Are the springs on these vehicles used in the same way as they are in the spring buggy? How?
- ⊙ What does the bubble buggy use instead of springs?
- ⊙ Do you think modern cars have springs or air pockets? Where and why?

Discuss what you think with a friend.

Get it?

What's left out?

p.41–42 **Read about Karina and Ben's buggy on pages 41 and 42 of the Companion, then answer these questions.**

Write the answers in your book. Use the writing mats on pages 62 and 63 to remind yourself of the features of recount texts.

1 Find three things that are different between the notes and the written-up recount.

2 Why did Karina and Ben make notes during the making and testing rather than writing a recount?

3 What information is given in the written-up recount that is not included in the notes? Why?

4 Find at least one example of something that is not a sentence in the notes, but is a sentence in the recount.

5 Can you think of one thing that Karina and Ben could have left out in their notes? Explain why.

6 Can you think of one thing that Karina and Ben could have done to improve their recount? Explain why.

Sort it!

How many?

Write the singular and plural for each of these words.

In your book, write:
Singular   Plural
(1) *straw   _____*

Singular	Plural
1 straw	1 buggies
2 bottle top	2 cartons
3 hole	3 distances
4 wheel	4 reasons
5 egg	5 axles

What do you think the plural of each of these words is:

cotton wool   **cardboard?**

Say it

Say it!

Why do you think ...?

p.41–42 **Using the Companion, in your group, talk about these questions:**

⊙ Why did Karina and Ben note the length of their buggy?

⊙ Why did they explain how they had changed the bubble buggy?

⊙ Why did they note down their predictions?

⊙ Were their predictions good?

⊙ Why did it make a difference that the back wheels didn't turn?

Change the text type

Read the recount below. It tells how a child made a magnetic car race game.

Use the writing mats on pages 62 and 63 to remind yourself about different text types.

I made a magnetic race track. First, I drew a track on a piece of cardboard. My cardboard was 20 cm square and it had to be quite stiff. I made sure that the track was at least 2 cm wide all the way round. I decorated my track to make it look like a real race track.

To make my car move I needed two little, round, button magnets. I put one on top of the cardboard track and held the other underneath. When I moved the magnet underneath the card, the magnet on top of the card moved too. I left my magnets on the card track while I drew a little picture of a racing car on a piece of card that was 3 cm square. Then I cut my car out. I stuck it on the magnet with a tiny piece of sticky tape.
I wonder if I can have a race with my friend?

Now make the recount into instructions.

⊙ Make notes so that you remember what you have to do and when.

⊙ Work with a friend. Make little drawings of each stage of the instructions.

⊙ Say the instructions aloud to your friend. Listen to what your friend says back to you. Can you improve your instructions?

⊙ Write the instructions. Use the instructions on pages 43–45 of the Companion as a model.

p.46–47 Read the story *The Experiment* on pages 46 and 47 of the Companion. Have you ever carried out an experiment that has gone wrong? What happened?

Sort it!

What happened next? And then?

p.46–47 Read these things that happened in *The Experiment*. Write the next two things that happened in the story.

Molly nearly listened carefully.

She got a tissue box.

She cut a circle of balloon rubber.

She used drawing pins to pin the balloon rubber onto the tissue box.

Say it

Read it!

Reading challenge

p.46–47 In your group, talk about why the author chose to use these words and phrases:

1 "Last week was our last science lesson with plants," said Mrs Kelly bravely.

2 Keep the egg safe? Was it in danger?

3 … like a queen giving out medals.

4 She made only a small hole in her trousers as she expertly cut out a round piece of balloon.

5 And strangely, time seemed to have stopped too.

Think about how the words make pictures in the reader's mind. Can you think of other words and phrases that could have been used each time? Explain why you like your ideas.

Draw it!

What is she like?

p.46-47 After reading the story, *The Experiment* in the Companion, draw a quick sketch of either Molly or Mrs Kelly.

Around the sketch, write some adjectives which you think of when you think of the character.

Here are some ideas to start you off.

nervous   brilliant   funny   hard-working
brave   perfect   expert   happy   sad

When you have finished, read your list aloud.
Can your friend guess who you are describing?

Write it!

What came first?

Plan the main points for a story about the science lesson we are told about at the beginning of the story *The Experiment*.

Characters: Molly and Mrs Kelly
Setting: a science lesson in the classroom

We know that during the story:

◉ Molly had been trying to keep her bean shoot warm;
◉ the fire extinguisher had been used;
◉ Mrs Kelly had lost some of her hair.

What do you think happened? Plan your story.

For your story, think about:

1 who the characters were (Molly and Mrs Kelly);
2 where they were (in a science lesson in the classroom);
3 what they were doing in the lesson;
4 what they were supposed to be doing;
5 what happened;
6 what the characters felt and said;
7 how the story ended.

Act it!

Topping and tailing

p.46-47 In the story *The Experiment*, the reader has to think about what really happened before the story began and what happened at the end.

Talk to your friend and agree what you think really happened, then try to mime it. Think about what each of the two characters (Molly and Mrs Kelly) is doing all the way through the mime. What are they looking at? Where are they? How do they both react to what happens? (You can swap roles so that one of you is the teacher in the first mime and the other is the teacher in the second mime.)

Enjoy it?

p.50–63 Read the three traditional tales on pages 50–63 of the Companion. Which one did you like best? Why? Was there anything in any of them that made you think of other tales you've heard or read?

Say it

Discuss it!

Culture vulture

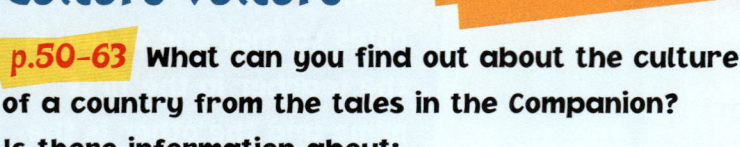

p.50–63 What can you find out about the culture of a country from the tales in the Companion? Is there information about:

- how children are supposed to behave?
- how men or women are supposed to behave?
- religious and cultural beliefs?
- what is important to the people?
- what the countryside is like?
- how families live?
- what people eat and drink?

In a group, discuss what the tales tell you about these, or any other, cultural issues and decide whether or not you think this is just in the story or in modern times. (Use some of the fact boxes in the tales to help you.)

Draw it!

Picture a setting

p.50–63 Read one of the tales. What is its setting? Read all the information in the story – together with any other information you can find about the setting – and draw a picture to show the landscape.

Compare it!

Aesop's Fables

Read these two traditional tales which are based on tales told by Aesop.

Find three things which are similar in the stories and three which are different. Was it easier to find similarities or differences?

The Dog and the Bone

Once, a hungry dog stole a bone from a bigger dog and ran off with it. As he carried his prize bone home, he passed by a stream and happened to glance down. There, in the stream below him, he saw a dog. The dog in the stream had a bone. A big bone. The hungry dog decided that he wanted that bone too. So he jumped, growling, into the stream. He landed in the deep, fast-flowing water and dropped his bone as he struggled back to the river bank. He stood there, hungry, cold and wet, and watched his precious bone being carried away downstream. Now the silly, greedy dog had no bones at all!

The Fox and the Crow

A fox once sat under the branch of a big tree. On the branch sat a crow and in the crow's beak was a long string of sausages. How the fox wanted those sausages! But he knew he would have to be cunning to get them from the crow. He looked up and said, "Crow! You are the blackest bird I have ever seen. Look at the colour of your wings!"

The crow was pleased, and flapped its wings so the fox could see them better. Then the fox said, "Crow! You are the most handsome bird I have ever seen. Look at the swell of your chest!"

Again, the crow was flattered so it puffed out its chest to look even more handsome. At last, the fox said, "Crow! A bird as black and handsome as you, must have a beautiful voice!"

At this the crow opened its beak, the sausages fell out and the fox grabbed them and ran off without waiting to hear the crow say, "CAW!"

Traditional story language

p.50–63 Copy the table below. Fill in the spaces with examples from one of the stories from unit 4 of the Companion.

Story title: *(Add the title of the story you are looking at here.)*

Language feature	Example
opening which includes setting, time and character	
ending which talks about the future	
connectives that signal time	
verbs to describe language, thoughts and feelings	
language which directly speaks to the reader	
'good' and 'bad' characters	

Sort it!

Verbs

Write the missing verbs.

In your book, write:

I am busy.
① You _____ busy.
② He etc.

I am busy.	I was writing.	I do my homework.	I have a plan.
You _1_ busy.	You _5_ writing.	You _9_ your homework.	You _13_ a plan.
He _2_ busy.	She _6_ writing.	He _10_ his homework.	She _14_ a plan.
We _3_ busy.	We _7_ writing.	We _11_ our homework.	We _15_ a plan.
They _4_ busy.	They _8_ writing.	They _12_ their homework.	They _16_ a plan.

Story themes

Think about traditional stories you know. What are their themes? Can you think of a story which has each of these themes:

- good wins over evil;
- wise wins over foolish;
- weak wins over strong;
- cunning gets you what you want;
- a quest or journey;
- a loss.

p.50–63 Each of these things and creatures appears in a story from unit 4 of the Companion. Which one? Sort them in your book.

In your book, write:

Skeleton-Ghosts	Boy who Flew to the Sky	Girl Stolen by Oni
horse		

Telling tales

Can you retell a traditional tale in under 100 words? Try it!

skeleton   drum   fire   temple   sledge

stool   black cloud   Moon chief   ship   cattle

spider   horse   river   mother   mountains

True or false?

p.50–63 Read the fact boxes for each of the stories in unit 4 of the Companion. Are these statements true or false?

The Girl who was Stolen by an Oni

- Japan is in the Far East.
- In the old days, Japan was a peaceful country.
- In the old days in Japan, men could not choose who they married.
- In the old days in Japan, girls and women always lived with their mothers.
- Onis are sometimes blue.
- An abacus helps you to spell words correctly.

The Boy who Flew to the Sky

- This story comes from Uganda, in East Africa.
- The people who told this story live near a high mountain.
- African folk tales tell of other worlds above the clouds and under the sea.
- The Chagga people live in towns and cities.
- The Chagga buy bananas.
- Ugali is a kind of vegetable.
- Some people think that if you have cows you are rich.

The Skeleton-Ghosts

- The Lakota people lived by hunting buffalo.
- Tipis were made of bricks and stones.
- The Lakota moved their camps when they wanted to find new herds of buffalo.
- Lakota boys were often good at riding horses.
- Lakota were always frightened of ghosts.

The Boy who Flew to the Sky

p.55–58 Read the story *The Boy who Flew to the Sky*, beginning on page 55 of the Companion, then answer these questions in sentences. Use information in the story to answer the questions.

1 Why did the boy's mother tell him to "Get out of here, go away!"?

2 Where did the magic stool take the boy?

3 Who brought the food to the Moon Chief and his children?

4 What did the boy need to make fire?

5 Why was the boy more helpful after he came home again?

6 Why didn't the Moon Chief immediately tell the boy how to get home?

7 The author uses the words 'cloudy' to describe the paths in the strange village. Why do you think she used that word?

8 Why didn't the Moon Chief's family eat cooked food?

9 The author writes about 'a secret slope where the sky joined the earth'. Why might she have called it 'secret'?

10 Why was the Moon Chief so grateful to the boy?

Say it

Say it!

Tricky words

p.50–63 All of the stories in unit 4 of the Companion, and some of the fact boxes, have tricky words in them. Try to read these words aloud. Think about how you knew what to say. Talk to others in your group about how they know what to say.

The Girl who was Stolen by an Oni

bridegroom
completely
priestess
mansion
guessed

The Boy who Flew to the Sky

Kilimanjaro
whispered
astonishment
ceiling
shrugged

The Skeleton-Ghosts

wrestle
actually
enormous
furious
dangerous

Sort it!

Finding plurals

p.58 Read the first two paragraphs of the story on page 58 of the Companion (beginning 'The things he needed were brought …'). Find all the words which are already plurals. Write each word in your book and write the singular form beside it each time.

In your book, write:

Singular thing	Plural things

Act it!

Character hot seat

p.50–63 Work in small groups. Choose a traditional tale from unit 4 of the Companion. Choose one person to be the main character. That main character needs to be able to answer questions about his or her actions in the story. Everyone else, prepare questions to ask. Questions might begin with phrases like:

⊙ Why did you …?
⊙ What was another character doing when you …?
⊙ What did another character do/say when you …?

Think it!

Character thoughts

p.50-63 Choose one of the characters in any story in unit 4 of the Companion. Look at all the different situations they found themselves in. How did they feel each time?

Draw a cartoon strip of some of the things that happened to the character. Use thought bubbles to show what they were feeling each time.

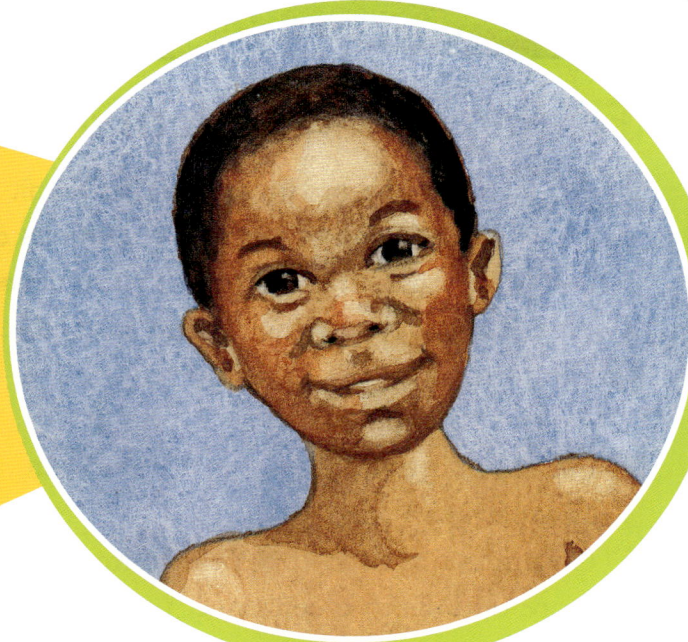

Draw it!

Character sketch

p.50-63 Choose one of the characters in any story in unit 4 of the Companion. Find all the information you can about the character ... then draw him or her.

Finding commas which do different jobs

p.50–63 Read one of the stories from unit 4 of the Companion. Copy down five sentences to show how commas are used for each of the following reasons. (The examples in brackets are not from the stories, but show how the comma is used.)

1 Commas are used before or at the end of speech. (e.g. *"I don't know," he said.*)

2 Commas are used after an expression of time and place. (e.g. *The next morning, …*)

3 Commas are used to separate items in a list, including two or more actions in a sentence. (e.g. *He slipped, grabbed my hand and …*)

4 Commas are used to add in additional information. (e.g. *his hand, which was very cold, …*)

5 Commas are used before an *-ing* verb. (e.g. *I walked upstairs, eating an apple.*)

p.59–63 Read the story *The Skeleton-Ghosts*, which begins on page 59 of the Companion.

Use these four sentence beginnings and write what happened next.

1 The first skeleton-ghost jumped out, YISSH! and blocked the boy's way, and …

2 The second skeleton-ghost said, "You have to dance until you die!" but …

3 The third skeleton-ghost tried to wrestle with the boy, so …

4 The fourth skeleton-ghost was riding a horse. Then suddenly …

Musical soundtrack

p.50–63 **Reread one of the stories from unit 4 of the Companion and think about how you would make the soundtrack for an event in it. What would the soundtrack be when:**

- the large black cloud took the girl away?
- the oni was slurping up the river?
- the boy was going up to the sky on his father's stool?
- the boy was making fire for the Moon Chief?
- the boy danced with the skeleton-ghost?
- the boy pulled the skull off the skeleton and used it as a drum?
- the chief of the ghosts came riding on his skeleton-horse?

Make notes to describe what the soundtrack would be like for each event in the story.

Can you make the sound effects using instruments in your school?

Enjoy it?

p.64–79 Read the letters, postcards and stories in unit 5 of the Companion. Which ones do you like best? Have you ever been to any of the places they talk about?

Cape Canaveral, **Florida**, **USA**

HMS Endeavour, **Java**

North Island, **New Zealand**

Churchill, **Canada**

Mount Everest, **Nepal**

San Pedro Town, **Belize**

Tristan de Cunha, **South Atlantic**

Kumasi, **Ghana**

Xi'an, **China**

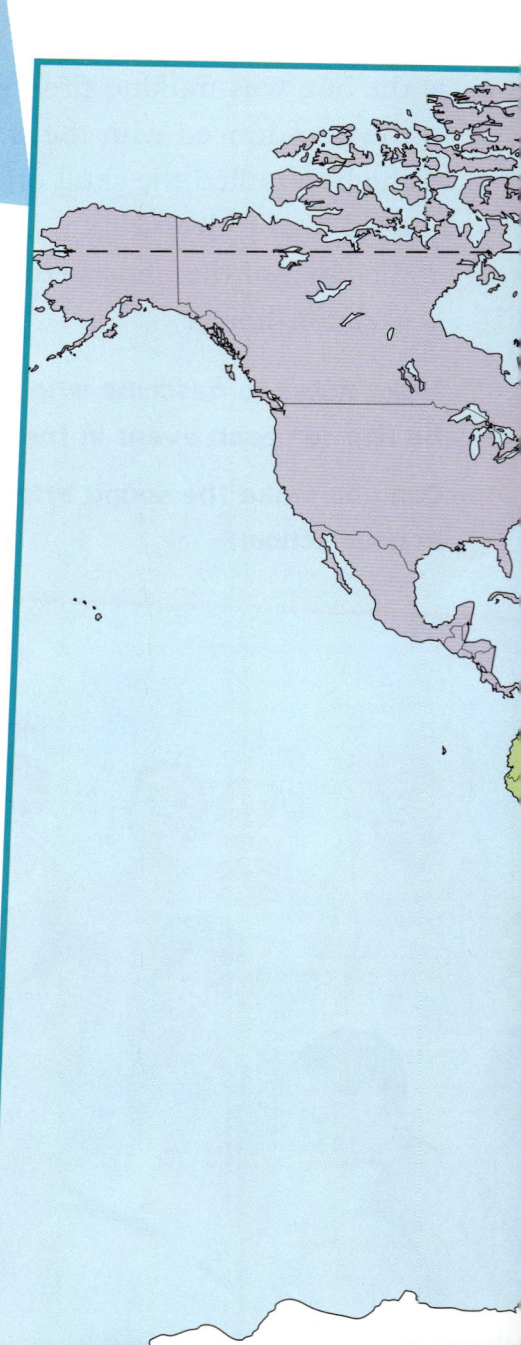

Say it

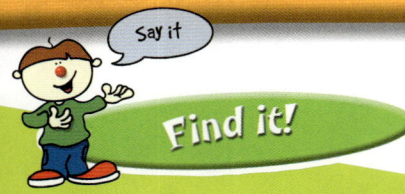

Find it!

Where on Earth ...?

p.64–79 **Use an atlas to find all the places mentioned in unit 5, 'From the Ends of the Earth'.**

If you haven't got a world map, you could copy or trace this one into your book and mark the places on it.

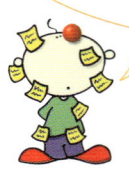

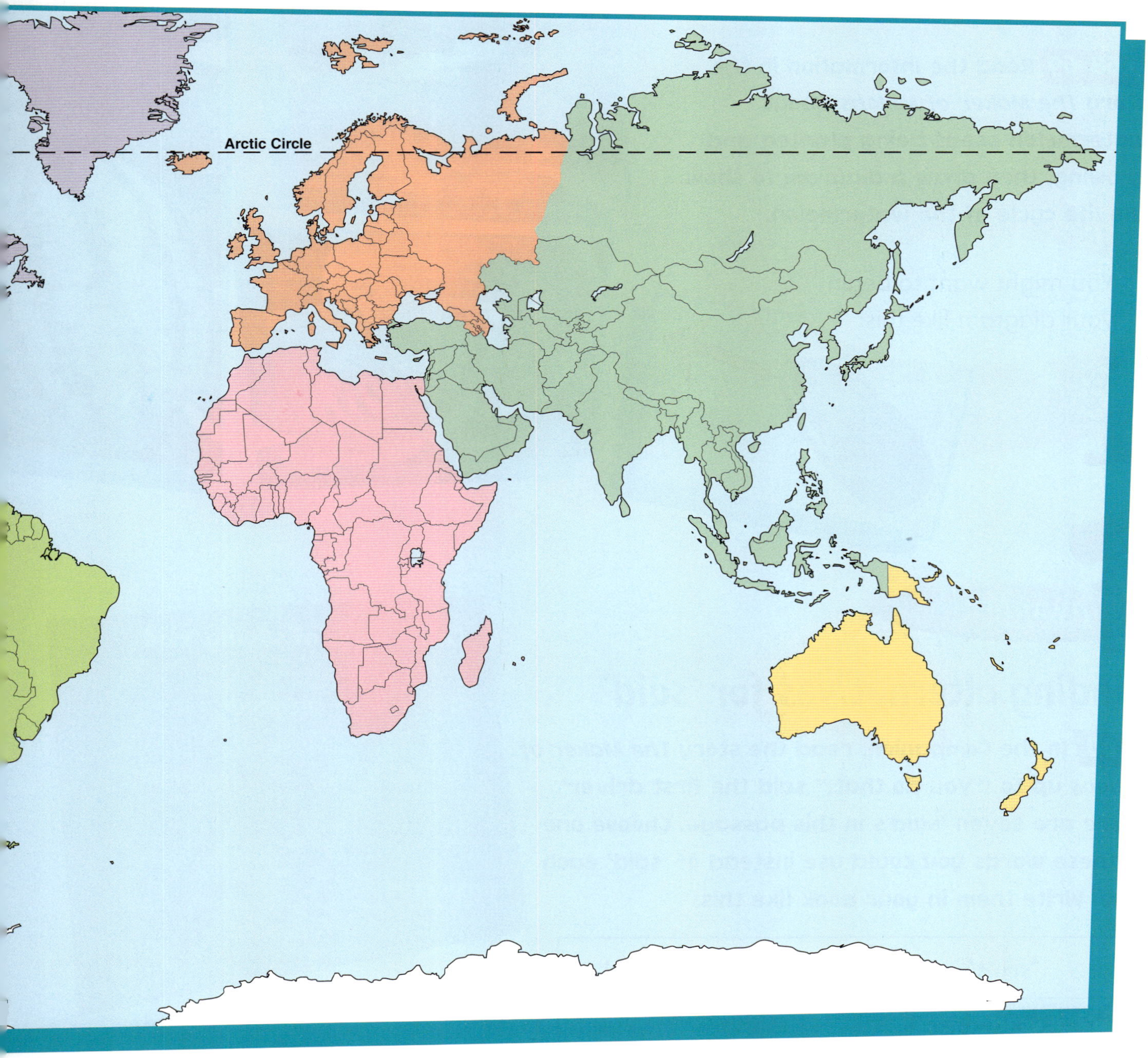
Arctic Circle

Enjoy it?

The Maker of Melons

p.68–69 Read the story about watermelons in unit 5 of the Companion. Have you ever eaten watermelon? Did you like it?

Draw it!

Growing a watermelon

p.68–69 Read the information in the story *The Maker of Melons* about watermelon seeds being planted and growing, then draw a diagram to show the life cycle of the watermelon.

You might want to begin your diagram like this:

Change it!

Finding alternatives for 'said'

p.68 In the Companion, read the story *The Maker of Melons* up to '"You do that," said the first driver'. There are seven 'said's in this passage. Choose one of these words you could use instead of 'said' each time. Write them in your book like this:

Other ways of saying 'said'

replied   pleaded   stated

requested   grumbled

shouted

answered   moaned

repeated   cried

'said'	alternative word
'said' number 1	

Discuss it!

Thinking about the ending

p.68–69 **Reread *The Maker of Melons* on pages 68 and 69 of the Companion. In your group, talk about the end of the story.**

- ◉ What do you think happened?
- ◉ Where did the old man's melons come from?
- ◉ Where did the melons on the cart go?
- ◉ Was it magic or trickery?

Talk about what might have happened *after* the end of the story.

- ◉ What did the drivers do?
- ◉ Where did the old man go?
- ◉ What did the farmer say when his empty cart got to the market – or did the drivers not take it?

Finding sequencing words

p.68–69 The story *The Maker of Melons*, has several events in it. For example:

| The old man talks to the drivers | → | He picks up the pips | → | He plants the pips |

Write a list of the events in the story, then see if you can find a sequencing word in the story which shows that the author has signalled it as a new event.

Act it!

How did they react?

p.68–69 Get into groups of three or four. Choose to be one of the characters from *The Maker of Melons* - the old man, driver one or driver two (or the narrator if there are four of you). Act out the story, thinking about what your character is feeling as the story develops.

Connecting connectives

Look at this list of connectives. Sort them into sets to show the kind of information they join together.

Opposite information

More information

Connectives

and   but   so   then   because   if   while   when   though   since

Sequence

Cause and effect

In your book, write:

Connectives that join up opposite information

but

Alphabetical ordering

Write these words in alphabetical order:

this   you   went   three   would   who
when   then   want   what   with   was
where   were   your   there   that
these   those   than   their

Writers and readers

p.65 Look at page 65 of the Companion. Read the postcards from Kate to her Grandpa and from Grandpa to Kate. Talk about these questions:

- How old is Kate? How do you know?
- Why did Grandpa talk about 'morning assembly'? What does this tell us about Kate?
- What do you think Grandpa was doing in China?
- What do you think Kate was doing in Ghana?
- Did Kate enjoy Kumasi market?
- What did she think was most amazing? Most disgusting?

Island email

p.78–79 Read *Island email* on pages 78 and 79 of the Companion, then answer these questions. Write in sentences.

1. Who is the email from?
2. Who is it written to?
3. What is there in the middle of the island?
4. What is the main town on the island called?
5. Why do you think Hari has sent an email, rather than a letter?
6. Is Hari having a good time?
7. Why is Hari on Tristan de Cunha?
8. Why does Hari have to go to the local school?
9. Would you like to go to Tristan de Cunha? Why?
10. Why does Hari use the words 'island prison'?

Get it?

Diving delight

p.70–71 **Read the *Letter of complaint* on pages 70 and 71 of the Companion. Use the table below to answer these questions. Discuss with a partner.**

- Which months are best for diving?
- Which months are the coolest?
- When are the seas rough?
- What can the wind be like in August?
- Which are the hottest months?
- When is the water warmest?

Belize weather for divers				
	Weather	**Air** Temperature °C	**Water** Temperature °C	**Comments**
Jan – March	☀ and ☁ and north winds	23–27	23–27	Rough seas
April – June	☀	29	25–28	Good diving
July – Sept	☀ and ☁☁☁ and ⇨	27–35	27–29	Good diving when sunny, but some hurricanes (especially in August)
Oct – Dec	☀	24–27	28–30	Diving OK

Discuss it!

Draw a picture postcard

p.64–79 **Read one of the descriptions of places in unit 5 of the Companion. Reread the description and think carefully about all the details you would need to include if you were going to draw it. Then draw it!**

Describe it!

Word search

p.64-79 **Choose one of the pictures from unit 5 of the Companion and write:**

⊙ five adjectives to describe it (adjectives are words that describe things, e.g. *hot, snowy*);

⊙ four nouns you can see (nouns are naming words, e.g. *sand, snow*);

⊙ three verbs you could do there (verbs are action, being or having words, e.g. *swim, climb, be*);

⊙ two adverbs you could feel there (adverbs can tell you how you do something, e.g. *slowly, lazily*);

⊙ one sentence using at least five of the words you have just written.

Write it!

Write a postcard

Have you ever been away for the day? Or gone somewhere on holiday? Or seen a holiday on the TV that you'd like to have gone on?

Write a postcard that you could have sent from this place. Make sure to tell your reader:

- where you are;
- what it's like there;
- what you're enjoying most.

Who are you going to send your postcard to? Think about the language you need to use.

Dear....,

Get it?

Pronoun hunt

How many pronouns can you find in the Companion which talk about:

me

he

her

theirs

yours

In your book, write:

he – his, him

Think about these pronouns:

mine
himself
we
them
you
yourself
him
his
they
themselves

Can you think of any other pronouns?

Enjoy it?

p.80–93 Read through unit 6 of the Companion and decide whether ...

- you prefer photographs, cartoons or other pictures;
- you prefer reading jokes, poems, tricks or facts;
- you think that it was a good idea to make this text alphabetical and mix all the different kinds of text; or do you think it would have been better to have different kinds of text in different sections?

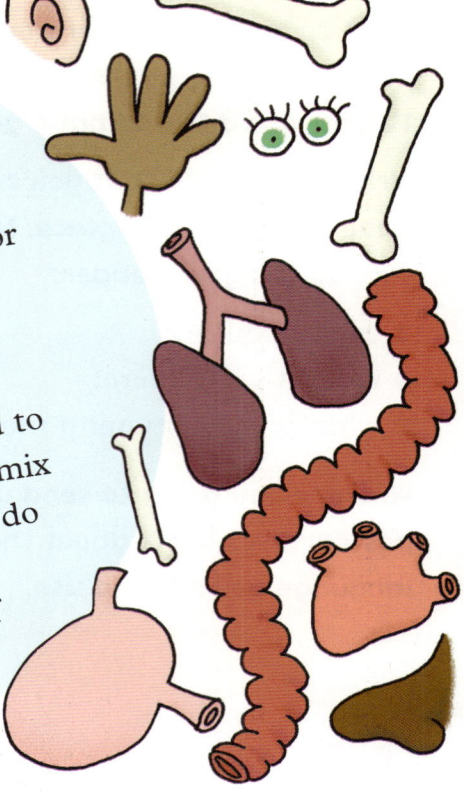

Find it!

Which page?

p.80–93 Using unit 6 of the Companion, write the page number where you can find:

1. information about lungs;
2. information about touch;
3. a poem about muscles;
4. a picture of a skeleton;
5. the fact that there are 50 million million cells in your body;
6. a diagram of a tongue;
7. information about your brain;
8. tongue-twisters;
9. a joke about a tummy ache;
10. a trick about touching pencils.

In your book, write:

1 lungs = page 86

Sort it!

Alphabetical body sort

Put each set of body words in alphabetical order.

In your book, write:
① saliva, scab ...

❶	scab	spot	shoulder	saliva	spine
❷	brain	bone	boil	blood	back
❸	freckle	fat	fever	foot	finger
❹	heart	health	hand	hiccups	head
❺	thumb	teeth	thigh	tonsil	tongue

Join it!

Body facts

p.80–93 Finish the sentence each time:

1. Your heart pumps blood around your body so …
2. Nerves run all over your body because …
3. Some people sneeze when …
4. Some areas of the body have more nerves than others so that …
5. Tendons are like ropes so …
6. Cells contain genes which …

In your book, write the whole sentence each time.

Find the information in unit 6 of the Companion.

Write it!

Summarising

Write a one-sentence summary of each of these passages.

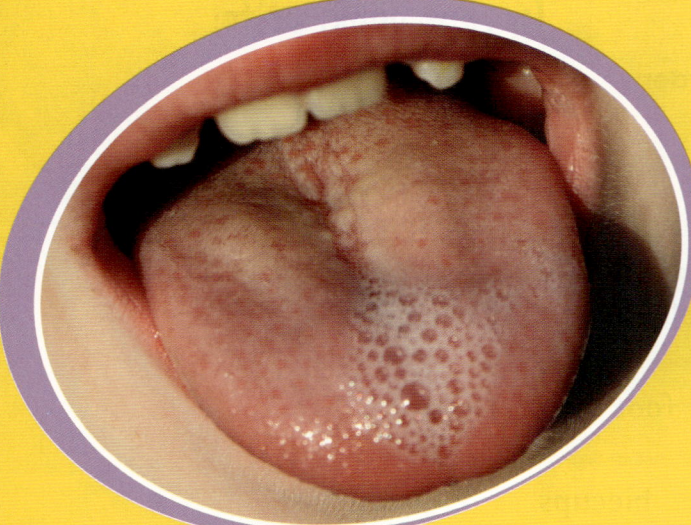

1 *Saliva* is the watery liquid in your mouth. It is also called spit. Saliva mixes with your food to make it easy to swallow. Saliva also keeps your mouth clean.

2 *Yawning* is a reflex action that makes you open your mouth wide while you breathe in and then out slowly. You yawn when you have not been breathing deeply enough to take in as much oxygen as you need. This happens when you are tired, bored or need fresh air.

3 *Exercise* is moving your body around in different ways, such as running, swimming, dancing or playing football. Exercising three or four times a week keeps you fit and helps your body to keep healthy and work properly.

Homonyms

Write the word that is missing from both sentences each time. It is the same word, but the meaning is different.

In your book, write:

① date

②

1 The *date* today is 14th June.
I went on a *date* last night.

2 A cube has six _____.
You shouldn't take _____ in a fight.

3 The film's _____ was exciting.
My Grandad has a vegetable _____.

4 Porsches are very _____ cars.
Cringed is a _____ verb.

5 Last night, I read a _____.
Did the referee _____ that player?

6 If you do exercise, you will get _____.
Do your new shoes _____ properly?

Endymion

The English poet John Keats lived from 1795–1821. He wrote many long poems and some shorter sonnets (poems with 14 lines, which have to have a certain number of syllables in a line and follow a rhyming pattern).

These lines are from one of his very long poems. Read the lines and think about the questions.

John Keats, 1795–1821

bower means 'a leafy shelter'

From *Endymion*, Bk 1, 1.1
A thing of beauty is a joy forever:
Its loveliness increases; it will never
Pass into nothingness; but still will keep
A bower quiet from us, and a sleep
Full of sweet dreams, and health, and quiet breathing.

John Keats

1 Line 1: does Keats think that beautiful things make you happy for a long time or a short time? Which word tells you the answer to the question?

2 Look at line 2. What does Keats think happens to a beautiful thing over time? How do you know?

3 Lines 2–3 tell us that, 'It will never pass into nothingness.' What do you think 'nothingness' means? Why won't beautiful things become 'nothingness'?

4 In lines 3–4, Keats tells us that thinking about a beautiful thing will make a special place where we can be quiet and restful. Do you agree?

5 In the last line, Keats tells us three things that he thinks are important in sleep. What are they?

6 What does Keats think will help you to have good dreams?

Fred's Head

Write a rhyming poem called *Fred's Head.*

Are any of these rhyming words useful to you?

bed, dead, fed, led, red, read, said, wed

Is this first line useful to you?

Once there was a man called Fred,

or ...

Write a poem that doesn't rhyme about your hand.

Look carefully at your hand.

Think about how it looks ... moves ... what it does ...

Shallow Poem

p.81 **Read the poem on page 81 of the Companion. Talk about it in your group. The poet is describing what it feels like to have an idea for a poem. Perhaps she had the idea when she was out for a walk and couldn't write it down!**

Think about questions like:

- how do you walk if you're carrying a saucer of milk? Mime it! How do you move? Why might trying to remember something like a poem be a bit like that?
- why is the poet carrying the poem 'carefully, nervously'? What might happen if she doesn't?
- where is she carrying the poem?
- the poet says that she might 'spill some lines'. You can't really spill lines of poetry, but what might she really do to them?
- which kind of pet do you think this poet might have? What makes you think that? If she had a different pet, how might the poem be different?
- in this poem, the poet is making a picture in your head, to show how carefully she has to remember the poem. Does having a picture in your head help you see what the poet means?

p.81 **Read** *Shallow Poem* **on page 81 of the Companion. Draw a picture of the poet thinking about her poem – or carrying the saucer of milk.**

p.91 **Read the poem *Dream Bar* on page 91 of the Companion, then answer these questions in sentences.**

1 What kind of bar is the poem about?
2 Which words describe the flavour of the bar?
3 What does the bar feel like?
4 How much does it cost?
5 Is this a real bar of chocolate? How do you know?
6 The word 'celestial' means 'heavenly'. Can you find other words which talk about heaven or the sky?
7 Does the chocolate make you feel heavy or light?
8 Why would this chocolate make you 'overcome gravity'?
9 Find two pairs of rhyming words.
10 What do you think is the best thing about this bar of chocolate?

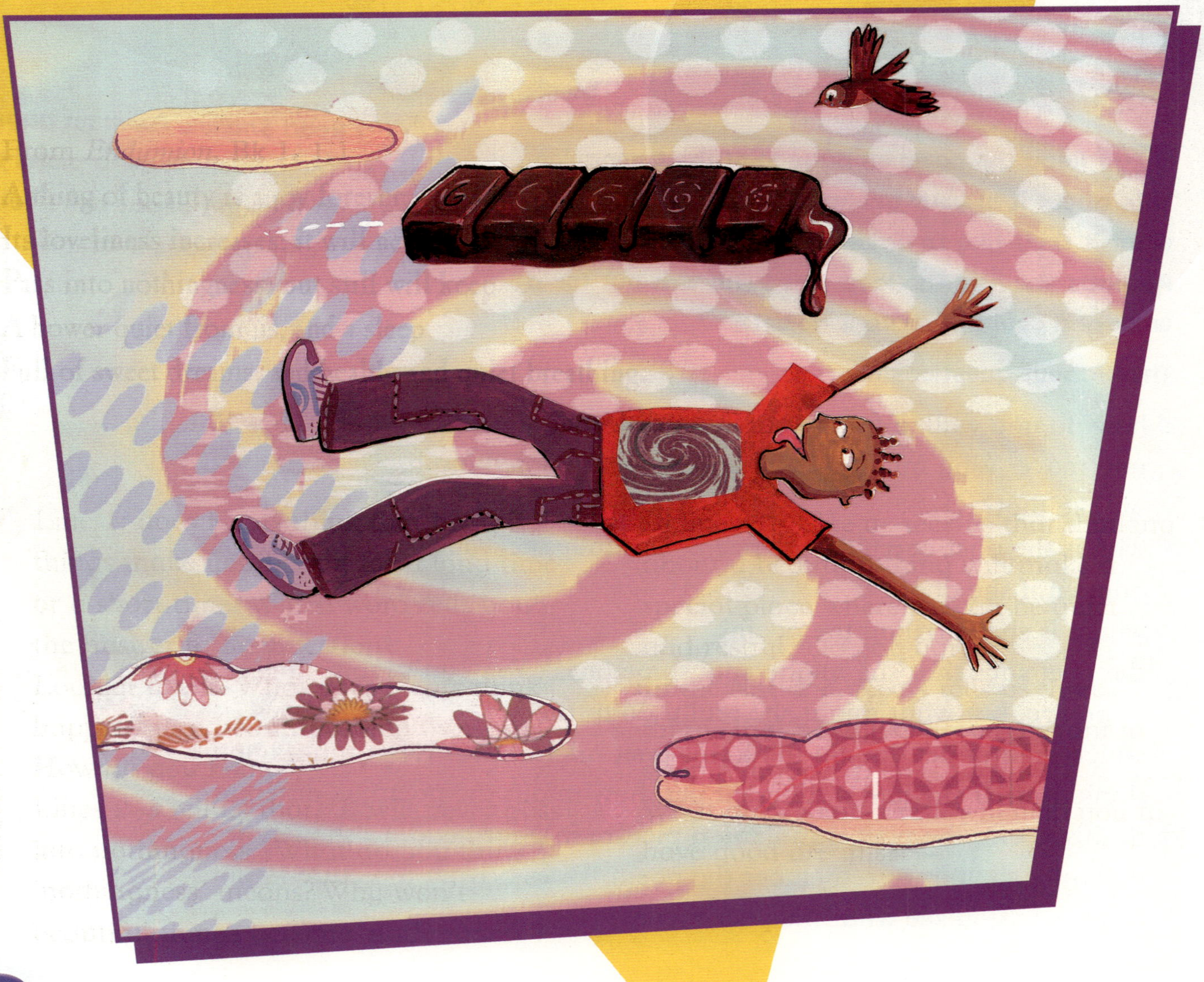

Read it!

Body bits jokes

Read these body bits jokes with a friend.
Do you think they're funny? Can you find
other jokes about bits of the body? Write
some of them down to share with your class.

Q: How do you make a tissue dance?
A: Put a little boogy in it!

Q: Why are false teeth like stars?
A: They both come out at night!

Teacher: You aren't paying attention to me. Are you having trouble hearing?
Pupil: No, teacher. I'm having trouble listening!

Q: What did one eye say to the other eye?
A: It said, "Between you and me, something smells."

Knock knock!
Who's there?
Eye
Eye who?
Eye've forgotten!

Q: What did the policeman say to his tummy?
A: You're under 'a vest'!!!

59

Words within words

In each of these words, there is another little word. Can you find it? In some words there are two, or more, little words! (Sometimes, remembering hidden words can help you to remember how to spell longer words.) Write the words that you find.

In your book, write:

brain – rain, in

brain heart stomach tongue

skeleton

hear tendon

muscles skin

breathe

Body organs

p.80–93 Which of these body bits are organs? Find them all in unit 6 of the Companion and list the organs. (Check in the Companion to see what an organ is first!)

In your book, write:

Organs
① ears
②

cells genes muscles skin

nerves

ears head stomach

eyes kidneys nose tendons

Body part phrases

p.93 **Look at the list of body part phrases on page 93 of the Companion. Which of them means the same as these phrases? Discuss with your friend.**

1 I can nearly remember the word.

2 Don't get so cross!

3 Haven't you got anything to say about it?

4 Keep going straight ahead.

5 It was very expensive.

6 I said or did something and I wish I hadn't because it's made so much trouble!

Writing mats

Use these writing mats to remind you about different text types.

REPORTS   *Purpose:* to describe the way things are

Structure:
- open with a general statement
- paragraphs begin with topic sentences
- headings and subheadings organise information
- non-chronological

Language:
- present tense (unless it's a historical report)

Slugs and Snails

Slugs and snails are member of the same family of molluscs.

Differences between them
The main difference between them is that snails have a shell in which they can hide, whereas slugs don't.

Similarities
Slugs and snails have many similarities. For example, both glide along on one, large, muscular foot. They both produce slime which helps to reduce friction so that they can slide along. You can see where a slug or snail has been because it leaves a trail of slime behind it.

INSTRUCTIONS   *Purpose:* to tell the reader how to do something

Structure:
- opens with a goal
- lists materials needed
- sequenced steps to achieve the goal
- numbers or arrows to show order of steps

Language:
- command verbs
- adverbs show order of steps

To make a cake

You will need: 2 eggs   125 g of flour
                     milk   125 g of sugar

1 First, crack the eggs into a bowl. Add the sugar and stir.

2 Then, slowly mix in the flour. Keep stirring while you mix it in.

3 Check to see if the mixture is runny enough to drop off a spoon. If it isn't, add a little milk and stir.

4 Finally, divide the cake mix between two 40cm cake tins and bake in a medium oven for 25 minutes.

LETTERS   *Purpose*: a variety of purposes

Structure:
- ⊙ address and date

Anyhouse
Anystreet
Anytown
AB1 2CD

3rd June

Dear Miss Brown,

- ⊙ opens with salutation

Language:
- ⊙ usually first person

I am writing to confirm the telephone booking I made this afternoon. I booked a splash party in the swimming pool for my son's 8th birthday. We will arrive at 3.00p.m. on Saturday 5th July. There will be 25 children and 5 adults.

- ⊙ paragraphs organise information

Yours sincerely,

- ⊙ signing off line

Mrs E. Taylor

- ⊙ signature (and name)

STORY STRUCTURE – most stories have five parts

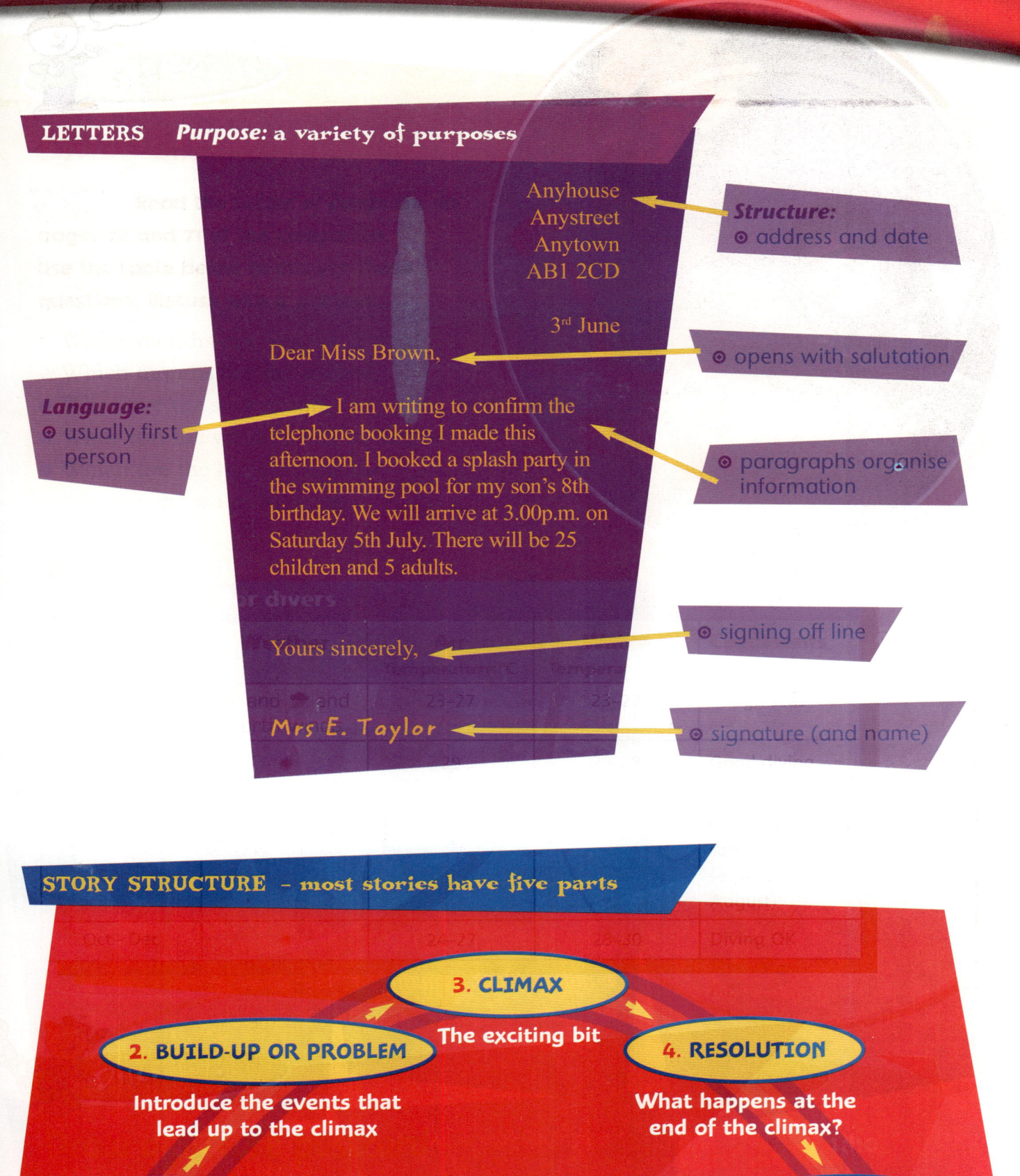

3. CLIMAX

The exciting bit

2. BUILD-UP OR PROBLEM

Introduce the events that lead up to the climax

4. RESOLUTION

What happens at the end of the climax?

1. INTRODUCTION

Meet the characters, Establish the setting

5. CONCLUSION

How does the story end? Is there a twist?

SETTINGS Function: to explain where and when the action in a story is

Features:
- In many stories the setting is important because it helps the reader to believe in the story, e.g. in mystery and fantasy stories.
- Settings can affect how characters behave
- Careful choice of words and phrases can describe a setting

Precise nouns
e.g.
- the ruin
- the glade
- the classroom
- the afternoon

Powerful verbs
e.g.
- creaked
- whistled
- smiled
- dragged

Adjectives
e.g.
- the _haunted_ ruin...
- the _enchanted_ glade...
- the _deserted_ classroom...
- the _lonely_ afternoon...

Adverbs
e.g.
- The door creaked _slowly_...
- The wind whistled _cruelly_...
- The sun smiled _cheerfully_...
- Time dragged _endlessly_...

CHARACTERS Function: act out the story

Features:
- If the reader cares about the characters, the reader will care about the story.
- Short stories need only one or two characters.
- We can learn about characters in different ways.

Looks like ...
e.g.
- freckles and a cheerful grin
- a permanent scowl
- hair as black as midnight
- a pale, arrogant expression

Does things like ...
e.g.
- bounced down the corridor
- glared at him furiously
- waved in a friendly way
- ignored her completely
- smilingly welcomed her

Says things like ...
e.g.
- "It's not fair!" she moaned.
- "Welcome!" he beamed.
- "Well, I don't believe you!" she declared.

Makes other people feel like ...
e.g.
- Horrified, she squirmed away from him ...
- She felt more comfortable now.